FUNDAMISM™

THE WORKBOOK

A workbook for creating more joy, FUN and fulfillment in your daily life!

PAUL J. LONG

© Copyright 2019 Paul J. Long
All rights reserved.

You are only permitted to use the content as expressly authorized by Paul J. Long or the specific content provider. Except for a single copy made for personal use only, you may not copy, reproduce, modify, republish, upload, post, transmit, or distribute any content or information from this workbook in any form or by any means without prior written permission from Paul J. Long or the specific content provider, and you are solely responsible for obtaining permission before reusing any copyrighted material that is available within. Any unauthorized use of the materials referred to may violate copyright, trademark, and other applicable laws and could result in criminal or civil penalties.

ISBN: 978-1-7343105-0-4

For bulk orders and discounts, please email info@fundamism.com

www.fundamism.com

"Fun is one of the most important—and underrated—ingredients in any successful venture. If you're not having fun, then it's probably time to call it quits and try something else."

— Sir Richard Branson

TABLE OF CONTENTS

GETTING STARTED	6
ONE: The FUNdamentals of Fundamism	9
Getting Outside of Your Head	12
Get Outside	15
A New Spin	17
Stretch Yourself	21
Listen With Intent	24
TWO: The Foundations of F.U.N.	28
The Foundations of F.U.N. Exercises 1-13	29
THREE: Next Steps to Even More F.U.N.	34
Foundation: Experience - Background	35
Foundation: Experience - Intentionally or Unintentionally	39
Foundation: Altering Experience	43
Foundation: Experience - Your Purpose	46
Foundation: Characteristics - Purpose Alignment	52
Foundation: DOPE - Your Bird Defined	55
Understanding Others' Perspectives: Experiences - What Are They Like?	57
Understanding Others' Perspectives: Experiences - Frustration	59
Understanding Others' Perspectives: Experiences - Curious vs. Furious	62
FOUR: More FUNdamentals of Fundamism	65
FUNdamental: Affirmations and Blessings	67
FUNdamental: Pay Compliments	69
FUNdamental: Listen to Music With a Purpose	71
FUNdamental: Exercise!	73
FUNdamental: Let It Go!	75
FUNdamental: Make Yourself Laugh	78

TABLE OF CONTENTS

FUNdamental: Medidate/Relax — 80
FUNdamental: Read — 82
FUNdamental: Stretch — 84
FUNdamental: Smile! — 86
FUNdamental: Additional FUNdamentals — 88

WHAT'S NEXT? 100

BEFORE WE GET STARTED

Identify someone in your life that consistently appears upbeat, optimistic, and troubled by nothing. On the surface, they seem to truly enjoy life and have FUN in all they do. Take a moment and recall that person . . .

Have you ever wished you could be a little more like them? Wished that you could let things roll off you like the water off a duck's back? Jump for no reason? Sing out loud without worrying what others think? Create games out of mundane tasks? Incorporate a little more FUN in your life?

Great news—you can! By working through this workbook (and reading the book Fundamism: Connecting to Life Through F.U.N.) you're one step closer to connecting to life through F.U.N.!

Vulnerability and acceptance are paramount in achieving growth. In order for joy and fulfillment to become the defining elements of your life, you have to accept and move forward from any past experiences that may be holding you back. Are you truly committed to creating change in how you experience life? Are you willing to do what's necessary to have more FUN in life?

> "We don't stop playing because we grow old; we grow old because we stop playing."
> — George Bernard Shaw

We all desire happiness and minimal stress. However, life doesn't care what we want. And, life doesn't always work out as we plan. To truly maximize life experience, all we can do is live with purpose and learn from our experiences—which is not the same as dwelling on them. The shorter the memory we have when it comes to those challenges we've faced, coupled with a strong ability to quickly move through painful situations, will help determine how joy-filled our experience in life will be.

Here you are—today, right now—taking the first step in bringing more joy, FUN, and fulfillment to your life. The thing you thought couldn't be done, you did. Challenges will continue to come. However, in working your way through this workbook you are preparing yourself with the tools and techniques necessary to combat the negative headspace such challenges create. You are moving yourself forward in finding your FUN!

USING THIS WORKBOOK

Firstly, props to you for continuing to do the work that was started in the book Fundamism: Connecting to life through F.U.N.!

The Fundamism Workbook is a guided resource to help you figure out your FUN and how to incorporate that into your everyday life.

The workbook can be used at any time of the year and should be referred back to often, particularly during challenging times, where fun might be the last thing on your mind.

While you can work through this workbook on it's own, you will get the most out of using this workbook in conjunction with the book, Fundamism: Connecting to life through F.U.N.!, which you can purchase from Amazon here: https://www.amazon.com/dp/B07JX7FTYM.

To get the most out of this workbook, I'd recommend you set aside 30 minutes a day to review an exercise or try out a tool in real life. Give yourself the space to experience more FUN and it will turn into a regular occurrence.

"You cannot build a dream on a foundation of sand. To weather the test of storms, it must be cemented in the heart with uncompromising conviction."

— T.F. Hodge

ONE THE FUNDAMENTALS OF
FUNDAMISM

I. The FUNdamentals of Fundamism

Picture this. You've had a rough day, week or month. Not so hard is it? What do you do to get out of that negative headspace to find happiness? Fundamism can be defined as the FUNdamentals of a FUN and optimistic lifestyle. Simply put, the principle is about gravitating more towards the things that give you strength as opposed to the things that tear you down. When we're faced with challenge, heartache or a bad day, it can be easy to sit in bed and pull the covers over our head. Feeling down and out? The snooze button is a little more common, negative self-talk begins to manifest and a victim's mentality can start to set in.

It is during these troubling times where you have to force yourself to do something that makes you smile. Maybe all you want to do is lay on the couch after a long and stressful day. However, living a life filled with FUN, joy and fulfillment is predicated on doing more of what lifts you up that what tears you down! You have to change your environment to alter your mindset.

The exercise that follows allows you to search within yourself to identify the activities that you find FUN. These could be things that you currently do, would like to do or used to do but got away from. No one else can define your FUN for you. Don't worry about what others think. Explore your inner child and come up with as many FUN activities as possible!

EXERCISE 1:
Challenge yourself to come up with five or more things you currently do for FUN (without depending on others) and write them down below. These are your FUNdamentals!

1.

2.

3.

4.

5.

Meditating, singing aloud, exercise, listening to music with purpose, enjoying a great meal, dressing up in a funny costume, going for a walk, and playing a board game can all be considered FUNdamentals. There are a million of them out there but not every FUNdamental will be FUN for you. No one else can define your FUN so write down only those in which you'd find joy.

How many more can you come up with?

I. FUNdamental - Getting Out of Your Head

What are we solving for by incorporating these FUNdamentals in our daily routine? As referenced in section 1, happiness can be elusive if we dwell in a negative headspace.

Individuals often ask how to shift a mindset from negative to positive. I believe the question we should be asking is how do we get people out of their heads? Individuals who consistently struggle with adversity, challenge or feelings of defeatism spend an excessive amount of time in their head. Worrying about how others may perceive you, what could go wrong, fear of failure or reliving previous experiences can keep you from achieving the happiness you desire.

Fundamism and its FUNdamentals are the solution to the problem of spending too much time in our heads.

EXERCISE 2:
What challenges, tasks or thoughts have been consuming your headspace lately?

Why do you feel they have been playing such a prominent role in your thinking? What is the importance of the items associated with these thoughts?

Best case scenario, what is the outcome you ultimately desire related to the challenges you've outlined above? Specifically, what solutions would provide you the mental relief necessary to move past these challenges?

What has it, is it, or will it cost you if you continuing dwelling on these these items without a course of action to move forward?

What excuses, justifications or rationalizations have you used to keep yourself from moving forward? In other words, what is holding you back?

Whether the answer is defining a solution-oriented strategy to solve for the challenges listed above OR finding specific FUNdamentals to help you move past them, what is the very next step that can be taken IMMEDIATELY to get yourself out of your head?

Now that we've identified the challenges, tasks and thoughts keeping you from the happiness you desire in life, let's explore some additional FUNdamentals that can help get you out of your head.

I. FUNdamental - Get Outside

> "THERE ARE MOMENTS WHEN ALL ANXIETY AND STATED TOIL ARE BECALMED IN THE INFINITE LEISURE AND REPOSE OF NATURE."
>
> - Henry David Thoreau

EXERCISE 3:

One popular way to mitigate stress and relieve the mental strife that life can present is to get outside. Going on a walk, riding a bike, exploring nature and throwing rocks are just a few activities that can be defined as FUNdamentals.

Name five activities (FUNdamentals) that you currently do that allow you to get outside and enjoy nature.

1.

2.

3.

4.

5.

Challenge yourself to come up with at least five additional FUNdamentals that allow you to get outside. How many can you come up with?

Implementation Time! Let's stop thinking about getting outside and actually do it! Take a look at your get outside activities listed above and identify a few that you'd like to incorporate now. Take the next step in making that happen, open the door and get outside!

I. FUNdamental - Get Outside - Reflection

What was your experience in enjoying the activities you identified to get outside? How did you feel when incorporating them into your day and would you do anything different next time? Did this experience spark any additional ideas that could create some FUN getting outside. If so, what are they? List them out below.

I. FUNdamental - A New Spin

> "THE WORLD AS WE HAVE CREATED IT IS A PROCESS OF OUR THINKING. IT CANNOT BE CHANGED WITHOUT CHANGING OUR THINKING."
>
> - Albert Einstein

EXERCISE 4:

So much life experience is created by the situations that we experience in life. Do you want more FUN in life? Create more FUN!

Stress, anxiety, discontent and apathy can often times be created by monotony. Doing the same thing every day over and over again can make you feel like you're in a rut.

Write down five things that you do every single day at home. Examples could include brushing your teeth, making dinner, watching the news after work or asking a loved one how their day went.

1.

2.

3.

4.

5.

Have you ever tried to brush your teeth with your opposite hand? Make a meal you've never tried from a recipe book? Watch Family Guy instead of the news? Ask a loved one the greatest memory they have from the day? These are all examples of how to put a "new spin" on things you do every single day.

Changing up the way you do monotonous tasks could help bring more FUN to your day and inject a rejuvenating energy into how you experience life.

Take a look at the five things you jotted down as activities that you do everyday. How can you put a new spin on them to make them a little more FUN?

1.

2.

3.

4.

5.

Now that we've taken a look at how to put a new spin on some of the activities you do at home. Let's explore how to create a little more FUN at work.

Write down five things that you do every single day at work. Examples could include checking your email first thing when you arrive, greeting coworkers with a hello, walking into the office or leading a meeting.

1.

2.

3.

4.

5.

Have you ever tried knocking out a to do list item BEFORE checking your email in the morning? What if instead of saying hello to your coworkers, you greeted them with some finger guns and a HEY! Ever tried skipping into the office? How about leading a meeting and incorporating song lyrics in your discussion without advising what's going on?

These are all examples of how to put a "new spin" on things you do every single day at work.

Take a look at the five things you jotted down as activities that you do everyday at work. How can you put a new spin on them to make them a little more FUN?

1.

2.

3.

4.

5.

How committed are you to improving the environment around you? The lists that you've created for putting a new spin on things both at home and at work are tactical behaviors that will create more FUN in your life. The only step left is implementing them!

Identify the items on your lists that you feel most comfortable in implementing immediately. Refrain from expecting certain outcomes. Go into this experience with an open mind and see what happens.

I. FUNdamental - A New Spin - Reflection

What was your experience in implementing your daily tasks with a new spin? How did you feel when incorporating them into your day and would you do anything different next time? Did this experience spark any additional ideas that could put a new spin on other daily activities? If so, what are they?

I. FUNdamental - Stretch Yourself

> "LIFE BEGINS AT THE END OF YOUR COMFORT ZONE."
>
> - Neale Donald Walsch

EXERCISE 5:

True growth and self-improvement happens when you stretch yourself through the initial discomfort. Think about all of the things you've come to enjoy in life. How many of them were you unsure about at first?

Make a list of things you were scared or reluctant to try but enjoyed after working up the courage to get out of your comfort zone and try them. Come up with as many as you can!

EXERCISE 6:

Look at the list above. Everything you wrote down represents a time where you overcame a fear or reluctancy and found joy as a result.

What are a few things currently that you've been hesitant or uncomfortable to try?

What is the mental block keeping you from trying them and what great things could potentially happen from overcoming it?

What is something that you can do right now to stretch yourself and move forward with trying a few? Go do it!

I. FUNdamental - Stretch Yourself - Reflection

What was your experience stretching yourself outside of your comfort zone?

How did you feel leading up to the event and what emotions came to you following its completion?

Would you try it again and if so, would you do anything different?

Fear, discomfort, reluctance, and negative thoughts are all feelings that can come along with try something new. These thoughts are very common and acceptable to have. However, to truly achieve joy, FUN and fulfillment in life you have to stretch yourself past those feelings to see what greatness lies on the other side.

I. FUNdamental - Listen With Intent

> "THE MOST BASIC OF ALL HUMAN NEEDS IS THE NEED TO UNDERSTAND AND BE UNDERSTOOD. THE BEST WAY TO UNDERSTAND PEOPLE IS TO LISTEN TO THEM."

— Ralph G. Nichols

EXERCISE 5:

Would you agree that there is a difference between listening to understand versus listening to respond? Which is more impactful in driving memorable interactions with others and why?

Provide a list of all the reasons why you could find yourself listening to respond rather than listening to understand. What could be getting in your way from being entirely present in conversation?

EXERCISE 6:

One way to enhance your ability to listen to understand is by asking follow up questions or digging deeper in conversation. For example, using phrases like "tell me more", "help me understand" or "please explain" might provide additional context to a person's line of thinking and make them feel you genuinely care. What are some additional phrases or questions you could use to get people to provide additional details in conversation?

Summarizing what you've heard in conversation can also show others that you've been listening and that you value their perspective. Your understanding of what was said would be provided before you add your thoughts or relay a solution to someone's presented problem. For example, you may use phrases like "based on my understanding", "what I'm hearing you say is", or "to make sure I'm on the same page" followed by a summary of what you've heard in the conversation.

Are you ready to be more present in interactions by listening to understand and showing a genuine interest in those with whom you interact? Challenge yourself to incorporate the follow up questions above and a summary of what you've heard in conversation before you respond to others for the next 24 hours.

Be present, be engaged and be genuine!

I. FUNdamental - Listen With Intent - Reflection

What was your experience implementing follow up questions and a summary of your understanding in conversation prior to response? What did you notice about the interaction and how others engaged with you as a result? Would you do anything differently next time and if so, what?

Now that we've established a few staple FUNdamentals to drive more FUN in life, you're ready to move on in exploring your personal foundation of FUN.

In the Next Steps chapter of this workbook, you'll find an additional 110 FUNdamentals. Are you truly committed to getting out of your head and/or improving your mindset? If so, see how many FUNdamentals you can incorporate and watch the joy, FUN and fulfillment in your life grow exponentially!

TWO THE FOUNDATIONS OF F.U.N.

2. The Foundation of F.U.N.

If you had to rate your ability to be deliberate in the things you do on a scale from 1 to 10, how would you rank yourself? Specifically, how often do you approach your day with a plan? In the space below, place your ranking and list a few of the items you find you approach deliberately on a regular basis. What behaviors or items do you believe you could be more deliberate with on a regular basis?

EXERCISE 1:
How deliberate are you? (1 being the lowest, 10 being the highest):

EXERCISE 2:
What are some items you approach deliberately on a regular basis? (Examples could include: morning rituals, team meetings, workouts, shopping for specific items, etc.):

EXERCISE 3:
What are some items you find you could be more deliberate in doing? (Examples could include: expressing vocal appreciation of a loved one, eating healthy, communicating with purpose, staying on task, checking in with your phone less, etc.):

2. The Foundation of F.U.N.

EXERCISE 4:
Who is the individual in your life that appears to have the most fun?

EXERCISE 5:
Describe some fun memories of this individual or examples where they demonstrated fun.

EXERCISE 6:
How can you incorporate some of these examples or behaviors into your life?

EXERCISE 7:
Which bird style best represents you? (You'll find more information about this in Chapter 3 - pages 57-60 inside the book, Fundamism: Connecting to Life Through F.U.N.)

2. The Foundation of F.U.N.

EXERCISE 8:
If you'd consider yourself purpose-driven, what is your purpose? (Having trouble defining your purpose? Don't worry, we'll help you as you progress through the workbook.)

EXERCISE 9:
How does your purpose manifest itself in the work setting?

EXERCISE 10:
If the people with whom you work were to describe you in three words, what three words do you feel they would choose?

EXERCISE 11:
How does your purpose manifest itself at home?

EXERCISE 12:
If your family or friends were to describe you in three words, what three words do you feel they would choose?

EXERCISE 13:
With the purpose you outlined above in mind and using only three words, how would you want ALL those with whom you interact to describe you?

IT WAS CHARACTER THAT GOT US OUT OF BED, COMMITMENT THAT MOVED US INTO ACTION, AND DISCIPLINE THAT ENABLED US TO FOLLOW THROUGH.

- Zig Ziglar

THREE NEXT STEPS TO EVEN MORE F.U.N

3: Next Steps to Even More F.U.N.

The following next-step activities will allow you to identify what drives you and where you go from here. They are structured in the same order as the concepts introduced in the book (chapters 3 and 4) on your foundation and understanding others' perspectives. Move at a pace in which you are comfortable. These activities should provide insight and will only work when you devote yourself to doing them right, not just doing them to check them off a timeline you arbitrarily created. This is your opportunity to be 100% honest and transparent.

Take your time, enjoy every step, and be as thorough as possible. Your ability to connect to your life through FUN depends on it!

FOUNDATION: EXPERIENCE - Background

The following experience activities are based on self-reflection. They require you to dig deep into your memory bank to answer the questions that identify why you experience life the way you do. Some of these memories may be joyous, others painful. It is crucial that you are vulnerable in the process to ensure the growth you seek.

EXERCISE 1a:
What experiences stand out as the most profound in creating your philosophy of living or "perspective" on life? Specifically, what experiences in your life have driven the way you see yourself, those around you, and your typical take on daily experiences?

3: Next Steps to Even More F.U.N.

EXERCISE 1b:
How did these experiences shape your perspective on life?

EXERCISE 1c:
What were some negative outcomes in your life that happened as a direct result of the perspective shaped by the experiences listed above?

EXERCISE 1d:
What were some positive outcomes in your life that happened as a direct result of the perspective shaped by the experiences listed above?

3: Next Steps to Even More F.U.N.

EXERCISE 1e:
What's the most embarrassing thing that has ever happened to you?

EXERCISE 1f:
Name a couple that models a loving relationship:

EXERCISE 1g:
What is it about this relationship you appreciate?

EXERCISE 1h:
How can the positive elements of this relationship be replicated in your relationships?

3: Next Steps to Even More F.U.N.

EXERCISE 1i:
What responsibility do you take in the creation of your perspective?

EXERCISE 1j:
What could you do TODAY that would allow you to take more responsibility of your perspective from now moving forward?

EXERCISE 1k:
Name a situation that's happened in the last month where you went negative. What could a positive interpretation of that experience be?

3: Next Steps to Even More F.U.N.

FOUNDATION: EXPERIENCE - Intentionally or Unintentionally

We either live our lives intentionally or unintentionally, and our overall experience in life is greatly impacted by this. Individuals that live intentionally typically have more F.U.N. and fulfillment in life. This is a direct result of being more present and having greater success in achieving the goals they set for themselves. These next few activities will help identify how deliberate you are in your actions and what steps to take to live a more intentional life.

EXERCISE 2a:
Your morning sets the tone for how the rest of your day may go. List the five things you do intentionally when you wake up in the morning:

1.

2.

3.

4.

5.

EXERCISE 2b:
What are some things you could do intentionally in the morning to help drive a different result in how you experience your day?

3: Next Steps to Even More F.U.N.

EXERCISE 2c:

List the five things you do intentionally when you get to work.

1.

2.

3.

4.

5.

EXERCISE 2d:

What are some things you could do intentionally at work to help drive a different result in how you experience it?

3: Next Steps to Even More F.U.N.

EXERCISE 2e:
List the five things you do intentionally when you get home in the evening.

1.

2.

3.

4.

5.

EXERCISE 2f:
What are some things you could do intentionally in the evening to help drive a different result in how you experience life at home?

3: Next Steps to Even More F.U.N.

EXERCISE 2g:

List the five things you do intentionally before you go to bed.

1.

2.

3.

4.

5.

EXERCISE 2h:

What are some things you could do intentionally before bed to drive a different result in how you relax or rest?

3: Next Steps to Even More F.U.N.

FOUNDATION: ALTERING EXPERIENCE

Taking the time to recognize what is driving negativity in your life and how your behaviors contribute to it can work wonders in driving change. The following activities can help shed some light on what is giving you grief and what to do to mitigate the sting.

EXERCISE 3a:
What is one aspect of your life that you feel brings stress?

EXERCISE 3b:
What behaviors or thoughts are you demonstrating that could be driving this negative outcome?

EXERCISE 3c:
What is one thing that you can do TODAY that could potentially mitigate the stressor you outlined above?

EXERCISE 3d:
What is another aspect of your life that you feel brings stress?

3: Next Steps to Even More F.U.N.

EXERCISE 3e:
What behaviors or thoughts are you demonstrating that could be driving this negative outcome?

EXERCISE 3f:
What is one thing that you can do TODAY that could potentially decrease or remove the stressor you outlined above?

EXERCISE 3g:
What is one more aspect of your life that you feel brings stress?

EXERCISE 3h:
What behaviors or thoughts are you demonstrating that could be driving this negative outcome?

3: Next Steps to Even More F.U.N.

EXERCISE 3i:
What is one thing that you can do TODAY that could potentially mitigate the stressor you outlined above?

3: Next Steps to Even More F.U.N.

FOUNDATION: EXPERIENCE - Your Purpose

Why are you here? What is your purpose? These are questions many struggle to answer. It's easy to get lost in the activity of our lives, putting things on cruise control and losing sight of the monumental impact we play in creating desired outcomes. By narrowing down the five core elements of your values set, you can begin to solidify your foundation and help identify your true purpose.

EXERCISE 4a:

Scan the lists over the next few pages and circle the words that aptly describe your values. Try to keep the list between 10-15 on the first pass. The next step will be revealed on the next pages.

Abundance	Boldness	Cooperation	Efficiency
Acceptance	Bravery	Cordiality	Ecstasy
Accessibility	Brilliance	Correctness	Elation
Accomplishment	Buoyancy	Country	Elegance
Acknowledgment	Calmness	Courage	Empathy
Activeness	Camaraderie	Courtesy	Encouragement
Adaptability	Candor	Craftiness	Endurance
Adoration	Capability	Creativity	Energy
Adroitness	Care	Cunning	Enjoyment
Advancement	Carefulness	Curiosity	Entertainment
Adventure	Celebrity	Competitiveness	Enthusiasm
Affection	Certainty	Continuous Improvement	Environmentalism
Affluence	Challenge	Daring	Ethics
Aggressiveness	Change	Decisiveness	Euphoria
Agility	Charity	Decorum	Excellence
Alertness	Chastity	Deference	Excitement
Altruism	Clarity	Delight	Exhilaration
Amazement	Cleanliness	Dependability	Expectancy
Ambition	Clear-mindedness	Depth	Expediency
Amusement	Cleverness	Desire	Experience
Anticipation	Closeness	Determination	Expertise
Appreciation	Comfort	Devotion	Exploration
Approachability	Commitment	Devoutness	Expressiveness
Approval	Community	Dignity	Extravagance
Art	Compassion	Diligence	Extroversion
Articulacy	Competence	Direction	Exuberance
Artistry	Completion	Directness	Equality
Assertiveness	Composure	Discipline	Fairness
Assurance	Concentration	Discovery	Faith
Attentiveness	Confidence	Discretion	Fame
Attractiveness	Conformity	Diversity	Family
Availability	Congruency	Dominance	Fascination
Awareness	Connection	Dreaming	Fashion
Awe	Consciousness	Drive	Fearlessness
Accountability	Conservation	Duty	Ferocity
Accuracy	Consistency	Dynamism	Fidelity
Achievement	Contentment	Decisiveness	Fierceness
Balance	Continuity	Democraticness	Financial
Beauty	Contribution	Eagerness	Firmness
Being the best	Control	Ease	Fitness
Belonging	Conviction	Economy	Flexibility
Benevolence	Conviviality	Education	Flow
Bliss	Coolness	Effectiveness	Fluency

Focus	Industry	Meaning	Prosperity
Fortitude	Influence	Meekness	Prudence
Frankness	Ingenuity	Mindfulness	Purity
Freedom	Insightfulness	Modesty	Patriotism
Friendliness	Inspiration	Motivation	Presence
Friendship	Integrity	Mysteriousness	Pride
Frugality	Intellect	Merit	Proactivity
Fun-Fairness	Intelligence	Mellowness	Professionalism
Family-orientedness	Intensity	Meticulousness	Potency
Fun	Intimacy	Nature	Power
Independence	Intrepidness	Neatness	Practicality
Gallantry	Introspection	Nerve	Pragmatism
Generosity	Introversion	Nonconformity	Precision
Gentility	Intuition	Obedience	Preparedness
Giving	Intuitiveness	Open-mindedness	Quality-orientation
Grace	Inventiveness	Openness	Reliability
Gratitude	Investing	Optimism	Resourcefulness
Gregariousness	Involvement	Order	Restraint
Growth	Inner harmony	Organization	Results-oriented
Guidance	Inquisitiveness	Originality	Rationality
Generosity	Intellectual status	Outdoors	Realism
Goodness	Joy	Outlandishness	Reason
Grace	Judiciousness	Outrageousness	Reasonableness
Happiness	Justice	Partnership	Recognition
Harmony	Keenness	Patience	Recreation
Health	Kindness	Passion	Refinement
Heart	Knowledge	Peace	Reflection
Helpfulness	Learning	Perceptiveness	Relaxation
Heroism	Liberation	Perfection	Reliability
Holiness	Liberty	Perkiness	Relief
Honesty	Lightness	Perseverance	Religiousness
Honor	Liveliness	Persistence	Reputation
Hopefulness	Logic	Persuasiveness	Resilience
Hospitality	Longevity	Philanthropy	Resolution
Humility	Love	Piety	Resolve
Humor	Loyalty	Playfulness	Resourcefulness
Hygiene	Leadership	Pleasantness	Respect
Hard work	Legacy	Pleasure	Responsibility
Helping society	Majesty	Poise	Rest
Imagination	Making a difference	Polish	Restraint
Impact	Marriage	Popularity	Reverence
Impartiality	Mastery	Privacy	Richness
Individuality	Maturity	Punctuality	Rigor

Sacredness	Sympathy	Wittiness
Sacrifice	Synergy	Wonder
Sagacity	Self-actualization	Worthiness
Saintliness	Strategic	Youthfulness
Sanguinity	Teaching	Zeal
Satisfaction	Temperance	
Security	Thankfulness	
Science	Thoroughness	
Self-reliance	Thoughtfulness	
Self-respect	Timeliness	
Self-control	Traditionalism	
Selflessness	Tranquility	
Sensitivity	Transcendence	
Sensuality	Trust	
Serenity	Trustworthiness	
Service	Thrift	
Sexiness	Tidiness	
Sexuality	Truth	
Sharing	Teamwork	
Shrewdness	Tolerance	
Significance	Truth-seeking	
Silence	Understanding	
Silliness	Unflappability	
Simplicity	Uniqueness	
Sincerity	Unity	
Skillfulness	Usefulness	
Solidarity	Utility	
Solitude	Valor	
Sophistication	Variety	
Soundness	Victory	
Speed	Vigor	
Spirit	Virtue	
Spirituality	Vision	
Spontaneity	Vitality	
Spunk	Vivacity	
Stability	Volunteering	
Status	Vision	
Stealth	Warm-heartedness	
Stillness	Warmth	
Strength	Watchfulness	
Structure	Wealth	
Success	Willfulness	
Support	Willingness	
Supremacy	Winning	
Surprise	Wisdom	

3: Next Steps to Even More F.U.N.

Obviously, no one can live by 10-15 CORE values. The very word core means the central or most important parts. So, the next step in identifying your true purpose is isolating the top values that are most central to you living life on your terms as your authentic self.

EXERCISE 4b:
Here's how—first, document all of the circled items from the above list. There are 15 spaces below for you to do this.

_____   _____   _____

_____   _____   _____

_____   _____   _____

_____   _____   _____

_____   _____   _____

EXERCISE 4c:
Next, isolate the top 10 from the list above.

_____   _____

_____   _____

_____   _____

_____   _____

_____   _____

3: Next Steps to Even More F.U.N.

EXERCISE 4d:

Then, from the top 10, what are the five from above that are most in line with how you see your life.

1.

2.

3.

4.

5.

EXERCISE 4e:

Finally, place a number next to each of the above 5 to rank them in order of how you live your life. Place them in order below.

1.

2.

3.

4.

5.

3: Next Steps to Even More F.U.N.

As a point of reference, let's explore a mock purpose exercise. Let's say I narrowed my list down to the following 5 words: (1) Care, (2) Energy, (3) Fun, (4) Happiness, (5) Helpfulness.

As you can see, there is some continuity in the words I've selected to define my core values. By examining these words, I'll write a purpose statement that helps align these core values to the purpose with which I live.

My purpose statement is as follows: My purpose is to reveal the opportunity that others have to have more FUN in life.

EXERCISE 4f:
Taking a deep look at the five core values that you've selected in exercise 4d, write your personal purpose statement below.

3: Next Steps to Even More F.U.N.

FOUNDATION: CHARACTERISTICS - Purpose Alignment

Your personal characteristics help create the experience and perspective in which you live. Exploring how you see yourself and learning more about how others perceive you can provide a better understanding of how aligned you are with your purpose. In addition, it may help expose additional growth opportunities.

Now that you've identified or are closer to identifying your true purpose, we can examine the personal characteristics that help support it. If you are living life with purpose, the characteristics you display should fall in direct alignment with the purpose for which you live. The following activity helps establish how close you are to achieving purpose alignment.

EXERCISE 5a:

If you had to describe yourself in three words, what would they be?

1.

2.

3.

EXERCISE 5b:

What experiences in life helped create the characteristics you model?

3: Next Steps to Even More F.U.N.

EXERCISE 5c:
Send an email to ten people asking them to describe you in three words. Review the responses and identify what behaviors you have demonstrated that could have driven their perception.

EXERCISE 5d:
Based on those responses, how would you say people experience you? Warm and fast, warm and slow, cold and fast, or cold and slow?

EXERCISE 5e:
What three words do you want people to describe you as?

1.

2.

3.

3: Next Steps to Even More F.U.N.

EXERCISE 5f:
Revisiting the purpose you identified for yourself in a previous exercise, how do your characteristics described by you and those you emailed fall in alignment with the purpose you outlined?

EXERCISE 5g:
What three characteristics would help drive or support the purpose you specified?

1.

2.

3.

EXERCISE 5h:
What behaviors should you incorporate in your life to ensure the characteristics you exhibit to others supports your purpose?

3: Next Steps to Even More F.U.N.

FOUNDATION: DOPE - Your Bird Defined

As discussed in the DOPE 4 Bird Personality Test section of chapter 3, The Foundation of F.U.N. (in the full book, Fundamism: Connecting to Life through F.U.N.), your personality plays a major role in how you experience relationships, life, and the creation of your perspective. Identifying the bird style with which you identify and understanding the elements of it can help answer many questions about your experiences in life.

The following activities will allow you to take a deeper look at your personality and how it drives your personal perspective. You can complete your personal bird assessment at www.richardstep.com.

EXERCISE 6a:
What is your primary bird style?

EXERCISE 6b:
If you identify with multiple bird styles, what is your secondary bird style?

EXERCISE 6c:
Based on the content in chapter 3, The F.U.N. in Foundation, your bird assessment, and your own personal experience, if you had to list all the characteristics of your primary bird style, what would they be?

3: Next Steps to Even More F.U.N.

EXERCISE 6d:
How might others receive or experience you based on the characteristics of the bird with which you've identified?

EXERCISE 6e:
What difficulties might result from these personality traits?

EXERCISE 6f:
What is one thing you can do TODAY to reduce the difficulties outlined above and potentially allow folks to experience you differently?

3: Next Steps to Even More F.U.N.

UNDERSTANDING OTHERS' PERSPECTIVES: EXPERIENCES - What Are They Like?

As discussed in chapter 4, The F.U.N. in Understanding Others' Perspectives, a person's perspective largely comes from their experiences. That perspective is a key differentiator in us as human beings. Now that you have more insight into the elements that create your perspective, we can explore other people's perspectives and the elements that formed those perspectives.

Have you ever encountered someone whom you really appreciate? Someone so memorable that when you walk away from them, you wonder how they came to see things the way the do?

This next set of activities are designed to help you dissect an individual's perspective and identify how you can use what you learn to close your own opportunity gaps.

EXERCISE 7a:
Identify the most FUN individual in your life (work, friends, family, acquaintances, etc.).

EXERCISE 7b:
What characteristics do they display that led you to label them as FUN?

EXERCISE 7c:
What do you know about their background or personal experience that helped shape the way they live life?

3: Next Steps to Even More F.U.N.

EXERCISE 7d:

Seek this individual out in whatever communication modality you prefer, compliment them on displaying the characteristics that allowed you to recognize them as FUN, and ask them what experiences drove their outlook on life.

EXERCISE 7e:

How could you incorporate some of the behaviors this person exhibits to help positively drive your perspective? (What is it they do that can be recreated by you in an authentic manner?)

3: Next Steps to Even More F.U.N.

UNDERSTANDING OTHERS' PERSPECTIVES: EXPERIENCES - Frustration

When was the last time you encountered someone that you didn't necessarily appreciate? In the following activities we will identify characteristics of others that may get under our skin and how to reduce the negative impact of interactions with individuals who display them.

EXERCISE 8a:
Identify an individual you feel brings stress in your life.

EXERCISE 8b:
What are the characteristics this individual displays that may rub you the wrong way?

EXERCISE 8c:
If you were to hold up a mirror, what is it that you could be doing in response to this individual that is driving what you see in them? How could your response to this individual be causing frustration in you?

3: Next Steps to Even More F.U.N.

EXERCISE 8d:

What can you do TODAY that will reduce the negative impact this person has on your day? Examples could include but aren't limited to: asking yourself questions about what could be driving your experience (curious); jot down the interaction you desire with this individual and shift your mindset going in; or have an open conversation with this individual about their expectations of the relationship in hopes of connecting on a deeper level.

EXERCISE 8e:

Name a time in the last month when you had a negative reaction to another individual.

EXERCISE 8f:

List all the possibilities in that individual's life that could be driving the way you experience them.

3: Next Steps to Even More F.U.N.

EXERCISE 8g:
How would you positively excuse the behavior? The bulk of people are inherently good, so how can you spin your experience with this individual to see the good in them?

EXERCISE 8h:
What are some positive outcomes of this individual displaying the characteristics they do? One example could include the following: you meet a physician who won't stop talking about how great they are and who expresses extreme confidence in their abilities. You are annoyed by their arrogance. Upon reflecting you think to yourself that if indeed you ever needed a doctor for something serious, you would appreciate having one as confident in their abilities as the individual you just met.

3: Next Steps to Even More F.U.N.

UNDERSTANDING OTHERS' PERSPECTIVES: EXPERIENCES - Curious vs. Furious

There are two ways to approach any situation: curious or furious. You may recall that curious individuals look at someone's behavior and ask themselves what could be driving the outcome. Furious individuals, however, look at someone's behavior and make judgments as a result.

As you interact with individuals daily, are you more prone to ask yourself what's driving their behavior, or are you more likely to grow frustrated by their actions? Below are some examples of curious and furious approaches to situations.

CURIOUS:	FURIOUS:
What happened?	How could they?
How did we get here?	Why me?
What led to this?	What the hell?
Walk me through ...	I call shenanigans!

Over the next few pages, you'll find three common scenarios in which you might find yourself. Under each, identify two curious and two furious approaches to the situation.

EXERCISE 9a:

Situation 1—It is one of those nights where you don't feel like cooking, so you take the whole family out for dinner at a local restaurant. Once seated, it takes several minutes before your server greets you. The server appears to be distracted and isn't very friendly. The food takes longer than expected, and once it arrives, it is cold. You eat at this restaurant regularly and have never had an experience quite like this one. How do you respond?

Curious Approach #1:

Curious Approach #2:

Furious Approach #1:

Furious Approach #2:

3: Next Steps to Even More F.U.N.

EXERCISE 9b:

Situation 2—You are working on a project at work that requires a deliverable or the help of another individual. Despite the fact that expectations were set, the person hasn't delivered on their task and the project is at risk of being delayed. You haven't had much interaction with this individual since the original agreement was made and need to reach out. How do your respond?

Curious Approach #1:

Curious Approach #2:

Furious Approach #1:

Furious Approach #2:

EXERCISE 9c:

Situation 3—You get home from work, and the house is in disarray. There's a huge mess in the kitchen, you can hear arguing in another room, and no one is ready for the engagement everyone in the family knows will start at 7:00 p.m. It's 6:15 p.m. How do you respond?

Curious Approach #1:

Curious Approach #2:

Furious Approach #1:

Furious Approach #2:

FOUR MORE FUNDAMENTALS OF
FUNDAMISM

4: The FUNdamentals of Fundamism

There are millions of things you can do for FUN to generate strength and distance yourself from a negative mindset.

By slowly introducing fundamism into your daily life, you will begin to see a shift in the way you view and experience your world.

Please note that if you desire to change your attitude permanently, you have to be dedicated to the implementation of this program.

Before you continue, you must ask yourself:

> Am I ready to make a change in my life? Am I ready to become the person I want to be, the person that makes a room brighten up when I walk into it or the person who can see what a gift life is and the difference I can make to others?

If the answer to any of these questions is yes, then you are well on your way to living a life characterized by fun and contentment!

Earlier in this workbook, we introduced the FUNdamentals of fundamism and examined the two, Get Outside and A New Spin. In the following pages, you'll find an additional 110 FUNdamentals to help create more FUN, joy and fulfillment in your life.

The first 10 give you in-depth ideas and ways to incorporate these into your life and the remaining 20 are brief thoughts and ideas to spark inspiration and ways you can take it further.

Try at least five of these over the next 30 days and note the difference they make in your mindset and improving your life's experience.

4: The FUNdamentals of Fundamism

FUNdamental: Affirmations and Blessings

WHAT:
Start each day with an affirmation and end each day by counting your blessings.

> "I'm in control of how I experience this day. I'm smart, funny, and have an uncanny ability to connect with others."

WHY:
The beginning and end of each day are of pivotal importance in the grand scheme of your life. The beginning of the day will undoubtedly play some role in setting the tone for the coming day, and the end will influence your bedtime routine and sleeping patterns, which are directly related to your health, happiness, and well-being.

HOW:
It is so important to start your day with some positive reinforcement. And who better to provide that motivational kick-start than you?

The beauty of affirmations is that they are 100% customizable. They are designed by you to help you motivate and applaud yourself. Do you want a promotion at work? Do you aspire to have more confidence when dealing with the opposite sex? Are you proud of any qualities that you already possess?

Ask yourself what things need development in your life and which of your traits you want to acknowledge or compliment (yes, I said compliment—if you can't recognize and celebrate your individuality, why should anyone else?).

Put together a sentence or paragraph that praises and inspires you, look yourself in the mirror, and say it with gusto! If you believe in yourself (and you start each day by reminding yourself of that fact), there is no limit to what you can accomplish throughout the day and, in turn, your life.

An example of this might read, "I am in control of how I experience this day. I'm smart, funny, and have an uncanny ability to connect with others. I commit to bringing more FUN to this day, and there's nothing that will stand in my way!"

We have all been guilty at one point in our lives of taking things for granted. We have also had moments of epiphany where we realized that we loved or appreciated someone or something because of what they add to our lives.

4: The FUNdamentals of Fundamism

In my case, those cathartic moments are generally followed by some guilt because I have not given the due recognition to those who have helped to improve the quality of my life.

In short, I have been remiss with regard to the words "thank you." Sometimes I am thanking an actual person, sometimes a higher power, and sometimes, I am thanking myself. No matter who is on the receiving end of my gratitude, it is important to identify my blessing and give thanks for it.

One example of this FUNdamental could be writing down a list of items for which you are grateful accompanied by what each means to you. By revisiting this list before going to sleep each night and adding or subtracting to it as you see fit, you'll find you are more present in identifying the good in your life and less focused on everything else.

TAKE FIVE MINUTES TO JOT DOWN YOUR AFFIRMATIONS AND BLESSINGS BELOW:

4: The FUNdamentals of Fundamism

FUNdamental: Pay Compliments

WHAT:
Pay a stranger or someone you do not speak with regularly a compliment.

WHY:
Dale Carnegie once said, "The kind words you and I say today we may forget, but the recipient just might remember them for a lifetime." When asking others if they receive enough recognition for the things they do, typically the response is an astounding, "NO!!!!!!" There is not a soul on the planet that does not enjoy receiving appreciation for the hard work and effort they put forth on a daily basis.

When you pay someone a compliment, you immediately see a change in their attitude. Smiles and a new confidence are usually the result of your kind words. It is not possible to know what everyone is going through in life or where they have been. However, by expressing your gratitude you might give someone the strength they were lacking to get through a difficult time.

While paying a compliment supplies the recipient with benefits, you also benefit! Your self-esteem will skyrocket with every smile you help to create. Relationships in your life will flourish as you begin to realize what an impact your ability to communicate has on those closest to you. You will start to feel a sense of accomplishment and joy that will help to carry you through even the most trying of times.

HOW:
We have hundreds of interactions with others every day. Accompanied with each interaction is the opportunity to express thanks. You might find that the young man working the drive-thru at your local coffee shop has a pleasant voice. Tell him.

You may be surprised by someone who waited several seconds to hold a door for you because they saw you walking up. Express a genuine thank you. Someone at work could be working on a cumbersome project and you notice the frustration on their face. Explain how beneficial their work is and show them appreciation for all of their efforts.

While the "what" in the compliment is important, don't forget the most critical aspect of giving compliments: the "why." You must explain the "why" in order to truly be effective. This can be done by expressing the importance of the recipient's actions or why they positively affect you.

4: The FUNdamentals of Fundamism

Below is a brief example of an effective compliment. We will use a cashier from a local grocery store in this example.

She greets you with a big smile and asks you how your day is going. She seems sincere in her questions, and you can tell that she cares to know the answers. You notice her name badge says, "Stephanie." You might say something like this…

"It's not every day that you find someone who takes such great pride in helping others. I just want to say thank you, Stephanie, for caring, and keep up the great work!

This FUNdamental is easy to implement as you have so many opportunities throughout the day. Start with one compliment a day and build upon your momentum. When your confidence starts to grow, increase the number of compliments to two a day.

The more smiles you help to create, the better you will feel about yourself and your ability to influence others.

Remember there is always a learning curve associated when tackling something new. You could be uncomfortable at first. It's OK! Continue to stretch yourself and expand your comfort zone.

With time and practice this FUNdamental will get easier.

TAKE FIVE MINUTES TO JOT DOWN WAYS YOU COULD DO THIS TODAY!

4: The FUNdamentals of Fundamism

FUNdamental: Listen to Music with a Purpose

WHAT:
Listen to music with a purpose.

WHY:
Music is a lot of things to lots of different people. I'm not a musician, but I wish I was. To me, music makes me FEEL. Anything I want to feel, I can find a song that will help evoke that emotion. Like many of you reading this, I can think of numerous defining moments in my life and associate each memory with a song. Below is the most impactful example I recall.

The year was 2013. I was living in Portland, Oregon, with my wife, Melissa, and our eight-month-old daughter, Adalyn Grace. The moment I woke, I checked my phone to find in excess of ten phone calls and thirty text messages. My father, just two weeks removed from his sixtieth birthday, had unexpectedly passed in his sleep.

A weird feeling came over me. I was numb and knew I had to make plans to get home to Kansas City to help my family in the grieving process while making arrangements for his funeral services. After exploring flights to KC, we came to the conclusion that driving would be more fiscally responsible than purchasing plane tickets.

We began our drive in the evening in hopes of allowing our baby girl some sleep to lessen her level of discomfort during such a trek.

It had been a day since my father's passing, and I still hadn't shed a tear.

It was pitch black as I drove through Utah with my headphones on as my wife and daughter slept in the back. My iPod, stocked full of 10K songs from just about every genre, was on shuffle when it happened.

Death Cab for Cutie's "I Will Follow You into the Dark" came on, and I completely lost it. As tears rolled down my face, I was taken by the words of the song and was forced to come to grips with the loss of my father. It was therapeutic, and I needed that release. Music gave me the power to FEEL.

4: The FUNdamentals of Fundamism

In a 2010 Los Angeles Times article (you can read this at the following link: http://articles.latimes.com/2010/mar/01/health/la-he-0301-brain-music-therapy-20100301), Harvard neurologist Dr. Gottfried Schlaug explained that when an area of the brain is disabled due to trauma or disease, music provides a unique way to reach that area, sometimes restoring impaired functions such as movement, memory, and speech.

There is also evidence that suggests that music can offer help to patients who suffer from pain, depression, heart problems, immune system issues and a rapidly growing list of ailments.

Is it not then a foregone conclusion that music has healing properties?

Perhaps we could even consider it a kind of medicine (a completely harmless and easily accessible medicine that we have unlimited access to 24 hours a day, without a prescription). Eureka!

So, why in the world would we not avail ourselves of this miracle drug?

While we are not exercising this FUNdamental to deal with serious illness, we are most certainly exercising it to engage our brains and provide a therapeutic and uplifting experience that can help us to relax, smile, or get motivated.

HOW:
This FUNdamental is super easy to incorporate into your day. When I wake up in the morning, I turn on the shower, followed by my favorite Spotify playlist. Depending on the emotion I want to feel, I have the selection that will set the tone for my day.

Every day, without fail, it wakes me up and puts a spring in my step as I prepare for the events to follow. My family also enjoys Hall & Oats dance parties, and we frequently have YouTube music videos playing at our house throughout the day.

Our children LOVE music, and we can definitively see a change in them when it's playing.
Whether you are showering, driving to work, exercising, or even relaxing at home, you can add a little music to the mix. It can act as an energizer or a relaxant. You choose the mood you are aiming for, pick some appropriately paced music, and it will do the rest.

Remember that the FUNdamental is "Listen to Music with a Purpose." I challenge you to choose your music wisely based on what you want to feel rather than just turning on the radio and allowing the DJ to direct your day.

4: The FUNdamentals of Fundamism

FUNdamental: Exercise!

WHAT:
Exercise.

WHY:
The bulk of society understands the physical benefits of exercising on a regular basis.

According to www.nutristrategy.com, thirty minutes of physical activity, five days a week can reduce blood pressure, prevent heart disease, lower the risk of stroke, reduce the risk of osteoporosis, prevent back pain, reduce the risk of developing diabetes, prevent obesity, and countless other health benefits.

What many people don't know is that exercising regularly can also play a significant role in developing mental stability and promoting overall happiness.

A team of researchers at Duke University recently conducted a study monitoring those who suffered from depression. The researchers monitored participants for a period of four months and found that 60% of those who exercised for thirty minutes a day, three times a week conquered their depression without the use of prescription medication.

The amazing thing about this study is the success rate in overcoming depression was the exact same for those who only took prescription medication! Millions of people spend countless dollars on prescription antidepressants annually.

According to this study, the same outcome of reducing depression could be had for free just by going on walks a couple of times a week!

British statesman, Edward Stanley once said, "Those that think they have not time for bodily exercise will sooner or later have to find time for illness."

Exercising throughout the week can promote not only physical health but will ultimately lead to regular smiles and a positive mindset.

4: The FUNdamentals of Fundamism

HOW:

You don't have to be a gym rat or have a monthly membership to an expensive health club to exercise regularly.

Anyone can spend five minutes exploring exercise techniques on the internet search engine of their choice to find a routine that can be performed in the comfort of their own home.

Regardless of whether we have a personal trainer, watch hours of late-night infomercials featuring P90X or Insanity, have our own Bowflex in the basement, or just go for a jog around the block, we all have the capability of getting our sweat on!

Exercise doesn't have to be as difficult and involved as we sometimes make it. Grab your iPod or MP3 player, step out your front door, and take in the sites of your neighborhood as you enjoy some good music and a peaceful walk.

TAKE FIVE AND PLAN OUT HOW YOU'RE GOING TO GET MORE EXERCISE IN THE NEXT SEVEN DAYS:

4: The FUNdamentals of Fundamism

FUNdamental: Let It Go!

WHAT:
Release yourself of negative thoughts, anxiety, or depression created by previous experience or heartache.

WHY:
It is an unfortunate, but true fact that we humans are plagued by negativity throughout our daily lives. Whether office politics, community problems, a fellow driver with a bad case of road rage, or a more personal issue has got you down, negativity is an unavoidable fact of life.

Fortunately for us, we have a choice. We can choose not to get mired in it and refocus our energy on happier things. We can choose to be forgiving instead of petty, cheerful instead of whiny, and we can move on instead of dwelling on adversity.

This is a multi-faceted FUNdamental because in practice, it incorporates both internal and external adjustments to your attitude. It requires you to stop indulging the part of your brain that wants to relive or obsess about bad things and to talk yourself into letting it all go. This FUNdamental, in short, is about being the bigger person with other people and when necessary, yourself!

Releasing negativity can change the tone of your day, and, in effect, your life. You will be able to enjoy work, social outings, and basic errands a whole lot more if you can learn to ignore people's bad attitudes and silence the discouraging noise the world is throwing at you.

Self-talk is an important component of exercising this FUNdamental properly. Patterns of negative self-talk are generally something that can begin as early as childhood. Not only do they serve as a vehicle for depression and self-defeat, but they can actually decrease our productivity.

So it stands to reason that if we change the pattern of chatter going on inside us, we can see real results in how we experience life on the outside.

HOW:
First, it is important to recognize how often you are contemplating or even anticipating bad things to happen over the course of a day.

4: The FUNdamentals of Fundamism

Once you have identified the frequency with which you incorporate these debilitating thoughts, you can begin the process of mitigating their control over you.

I am of the opinion that if you say something enough, you can talk yourself into believing it. Therefore, the more you tell yourself bad things are going to happen, the more you experience bad things happening!

Oftentimes, great things are happening all around you, but you don't even notice if you've trained your brain to expect only negativity.

So how do you change?

We first need to replace those negative thoughts with positive ones. Take notice of how you are phrasing things and make note of them in a journal.

Are you using a lot of phrases like "I can't," "I won't," or "I don't"? Turn those negative statements into motivating questions. For instance, "I can't do this" can be changed to "How can I do this?" If negative self-talk is creating outcomes that generate misery, rephrasing statements to drive a more positive mindset is key to delivering a different life experience.

Another important aspect of this FUNdamental is letting go of things that persistently plague you. While past experiences can prove powerful learning tools in avoiding previous mistakes, it is hard to move forward if you're consistently looking in the rearview mirror. Life is full of challenges. Some are far worse than others.

Whether you've experienced the terrible loss of a loved one, a traumatic event, made a terrible decision, fell out with a friend, or anything else that is consistently weighing heavily on your mind, you have to let it go.

Take time to grieve, think about what you learned from the experience, even provide yourself time to appreciate the greatness that was offered as a result of that individual or situation—and then LET IT GO!

4: The FUNdamentals of Fundamism

Think about one individual you haven't communicated with in a while. They were once a close friend, family member, or someone with whom you enjoyed interacting.

For some reason, you stopped. You had a disagreement, they said something you didn't like, or something came between you. Let it go.

Pick up your phone right now and drop them a line. Text, call, or email this individual, and tell them you're thinking of them and the fun they once brought to your life. Do so without expectation of how, if, or when they respond, and feel the release of an old hurt.

In closing, there is no way to avoid negativity altogether. However, if you practice the Let It Go FUNdamental, confining these negative experiences to short-term memory and incorporating some positive self-talk, you'll be in awe how differently you'll experience life.

So LET IT GO ALREADY!

TAKE FIVE MINUTES TO WRITE DOWN WHAT YOU NEED TO LET GO RIGHT NOW:

4: The FUNdamentals of Fundamism

FUNdamental: Make Yourself Laugh

WHAT:
Find ways to make yourself laugh.

WHY:
"Humor is the great thing, the saving thing. The minute it crops up, all of our irritations and resentments slip away and a sunny spirit takes their place." —Mark Twain

While many of us have heard that laughter is the best medicine for what ails us, I believe Mark Twain truly captured the definition of humor and how it positively affects us in his quote above.

According to Paul E. McGhee, PhD, "Your sense of humor is one of the most powerful tools you have to make certain your daily mood and emotional state support good health."

Those that laugh regularly know that it helps spark energy, regulates pain, reduces stress, and even strengthens the immune system!

Laughter is contagious. When one person laughs, others tend to follow suit. No one wants to be the person that gets others down. Humor is one sure fire way to positively impact not only yourself but others, as well.

HOW:
There are countless ways to make yourself or others laugh. Sharing embarrassing moments, telling jokes, doing silly dances with friends, or watching comedy television are just a few ways to get that funny bone tickled.

Every Friday night on Comedy Central, stand-up comics perform on a show called "Comedy Central Presents." By setting my DVR recorder to record this entire series, I can generate a laugh whenever I need to just by pressing "play."

Another avenue to explore when trying to get a chuckle is to laugh at yourself. There is no better time to act ridiculous than when no one else is around. When we are alone, no one is around to judge us but ourselves.

4: The FUNdamentals of Fundamism

For years, I worked as a call center representative who had to fix people's "problems" on a daily basis. It seemed as though everyone who called me was mad at the world and needed me to turn their situation around.

Hearing negative experiences day in and day out can really take a toll on an individual's mindset. Following a long and tiresome day, I would always try to find ways to cleanse myself of the negativity that surrounded me at work.

One of my favorite ways of accomplishing this was to drop my things at the door upon my arrival home and sprint to my bedroom. Once my bed was in sight, I would leap onto it with my arms and legs fully extended.

Those of you familiar with wrestling may remember a wrestler by the name of Eddie Guerrero. It was his move known only as "the frog splash" that turned my day around.

You see, when I dropped my "baggage" at the door and made the leap into my bed, I felt silly. I even remember saying out loud, "Paul, you're an idiot!" However, no one was around to judge me, and ultimately, I felt completely different about myself and my day. It was as though I had taken a bath in positivity!

Other ways that have helped me to laugh at myself are dancing before the mirror, making up songs, and talking to myself. I don't believe that there is any one way that is better than another for the implementation of this FUNdamental.

If it makes you laugh, then do it often!

TAKE FIVE MINUTES TO JOT DOWN HOW YOU CAN "MAKE YOURSELF LAUGH" TODAY:

4: The FUNdamentals of Fundamism

FUNdamental: Meditate/Relax

WHAT:
Take time out of your busy day to relax or meditate.

WHY:
Have you ever laid down for bed at the end of a busy day and were unable to sleep as your brain was overwhelmed with thoughts of things to do or worries out of your control? Join the club!

One can argue that the reason this happens is due to the fact that we are always preoccupied with the things going on throughout our day. When we don't take time to ourselves to clear our minds and focus solely on our own personal well-being, our brain takes over when our day slows down. This, of course, usually being the time we lay ourselves down to sleep.

Per an article written by Psychology Today called, "The Benefits of Meditation," those that meditate "shift negative brain waves in the stress prone right frontal cortex of the brain to the calmer left frontal cortex."

Unfortunately, I am no doctor so I struggle understanding what this statement means. Luckily the article breaks it down to explain that when you meditate, a mental shift happens in the brain such that there's a significant reduction in the likelihood of stress, anxiety, and depression.

HOW:
There are numerous resources in the world today dedicated to meditation including the how to, benefits of, and whys surrounding its value. A couple of our favorites are Stephan Bodian's Meditation for Dummies and Victor Davich's 8 Minute Meditation.

Meditation for Dummies includes an audio CD with short meditation exercises that you can download to an iPod or MP3 player. You can do these exercises when you awake from your slumber, in the sauna at the gym, during lunch in the office, or right before bed.

8 Minute Meditation focuses on meditation for the beginner and those constantly on the run. The book quickly gives you exercises and explains why they are important. It allows you to experience the power of meditation simply by doing.

4: The FUNdamentals of Fundamism

The only way to believe in something is to experience it ourselves. 8 Minute Mediation allows you the chance to determine whether meditation is right for you in minutes.

As I am not a meditation expert, I don't want to give too much info on how to meditate. However, a good friend of mine painted a picture of how he incorporates meditation in his daily life.

Below you will find his instruction:

- Find a quiet place where you will not be interrupted, and get comfortable.
- Close your eyes and focus on your breathing. Feel the oxygen fill your lungs.
- As you exhale, imagine letting go of all the anxiety and worry in your life.
- While continuing to focus on your breath, picture yourself floating to the bottom of a body of water. As your weighted body sinks further down, look up to where you originally entered the water.
- Picture your worry and the troubles in your life getting further and further away from you as you left them when you took the plunge.
- Breathe easy and continue to focus on the oxygen entering and filling your body. As you plummet further into the water, embrace the clarity of your mind as your thoughts are left far above you.

Remember what Travis Kelce stated in the foreword of the book?

"As you reflect, find comfort in revisiting the past. Yes, you'll feel some pain but reliving how you felt through your worst moments can help keep you on track. It keeps your mind in a place where you're motivated to make sure you never get back to that point again.

The key to growth is pushing through the heartache without wallowing in it and developing a plan to move yourself forward."

While meditating, embrace your thoughts as they help identify your foundation, then work to clear your mind of all things so as to find the right path to your own enlightenment.

4: The FUNdamentals of Fundamism

FUNdamental: Read

WHAT:
Read something of interest.

WHY:
When I was a kid, my mother always told me that reading made me smart. For years I thought intelligence was directly correlated to the number of books I read.

Maybe that's why Forrest Gump's "I'm not a smart man" quote always resonated with me. Dr. Seuss once wrote, "The more that you read, the more things you will know. The more that you learn, the more places you'll go." I knew that reading would provide me opportunity, but it was not something that I enjoyed or gave me strength. As a result, I found myself gravitating towards other FUNdamentals like working out, video games, playing basketball, and more.

As I grew older, I realized that there are far more benefits to reading than just growing my vocabulary or feeling smart, mental health being the most important to me.

A 2013 article from The Atlantic titled, "More Scientific Evidence That Reading Is Good for You," details how reading reduced the rate of cognitive decline in dementia patients. In addition, the article outlines how reading can provide individuals with "an increased tolerance for uncertainty."

One of the most powerful articles on the benefits of reading for me was a Huffington Post column titled, "6 Science-Backed Reasons to Go Read a Book Right Now," written by Laura Schocker.

Laura stated that reading can reduce stress, keep the brain sharp, reduce the risk of Alzheimer's disease, help you sleep better, make you more empathetic, and ease depression.
What more evidence do we need?

I know reading is not always as F.U.N. as binge watching Netflix. However, if reading can improve mental health as outlined above, why not give it a try?

HOW:
There are millions of pieces of literature that can be found anywhere including the checkout counter at a local grocery store, the library, or at the click of a button from the comfort of your own home.

4: The FUNdamentals of Fundamism

My mother, Martha, goes to the library every Saturday morning, checks out three novels, reads them all in a week's time, and returns them the following Saturday to repeat the cycle.

I'm not that diligent or driven to read at that level. Typically, I enjoy reading sports, feel-good stories, or news articles from links I find on Twitter.

For me, it's important to avoid strongly opinionated articles or those written with a negative tone. As a motivational speaker, I always thought I had to read self-help content to stay relevant in my industry. However, when I read that type of content, typically I lose interest within minutes.

As you begin or continue your exploration into the FUNdamental of reading, it's imperative that you balance the things you think you should read with those that are actually of interest. This will improve the likelihood of you enjoying reading while reducing the probability of burnout.

Tonight as you finally find time to wind down and are looking for a little mental relief, try substituting the remote for a good read. If the result is a great night's rest and a temporary escape from your troubles, you'll be thankful you did.

TAKE FIVE MINUTES TO JOT DOWN THE NEXT THREE ITEMS YOU'RE GOING TO READ:

4: The FUNdamentals of Fundamism

FUNdamental: Stretch

WHAT:
Get your stretch on or try some yoga.

WHY:
Now I'm not the most flexible gentleman on the planet. However, when I get a good stretch in, I typically end up feeling more relaxed, mentally fit, and at peace with my surroundings. After three knee surgeries, I've found that stretching can ease the pain created by changes in weather pressure or physical activity.

Being more bendy is an added bonus, if you get my drift.

K. Aleisha Fetters, in her Fitness Magazine column titled, "11 Seriously Awesome Benefits of Stretching," wrote that, "stretching primes your muscles for exercise, improves your posture, eases back pain, improves exercise form, prevents injury, boosts joint health, slashes stress, helps you sleep better, boosts blood flow to your brain, improves energy, and fights nagging anxieties."

Oftentimes we consider stretching as a precursor to an activity or something to be incorporated after exercise. As you can see from the benefits above, stretching doesn't have to apply exclusively to pre-or post-workouts. Stretching itself can be the activity.

Challenge yourself to a good stretch and feel the difference in your physical and mental health!

HOW:
Try touching your toes (just give your legs a hug if you can't), bring your knees to your chest while lying on the floor, make a butterfly with your legs to stretch the groin, grab your elbow over your head to stretch your triceps, and grab a door jam stretching your arm behind you to work those pectorals.

There are a million resources out there for guidance on stretching.

Take a yoga class, check out a book from the library, or do an old-fashioned internet search on "easy stretches."

4: The FUNdamentals of Fundamism

Grab a family member, coworker, or friend to give you a hand, and don't push yourself too hard. You'll want to feel some sensation but not excruciating pain. Thirty to forty-five seconds per stretch and just two or three stretches total is typically a good way to get the blood flowing.

If you're not used to stretching, be patient with yourself. As stated before, I'm not the most flexible.

However, setting aside a few minutes a day to get my stretch on has produced countless benefits, and I'm getting more limber by the day.

Have F.U.N. and happy stretching!

TAKE FIVE MINUTES TO PLAN HOW YOU'LL FIT IN STRETCHING OR YOGA INTO YOUR WEEK:

4: The FUNdamentals of Fundamism

FUNdamental: Smile!

WHAT:
Make yourself smile.

WHY:
Bobby McFerrin once sang, "Don't worry, be happy. Cause when you worry, your face will frown and that will bring everybody down, so don't worry, be happy (now)." It was a popular and uplifting song for a very specific reason.

Though a smile isn't generally going to be a cure-all for what's nagging at you, the domino effect of the impression it leaves on others can actually make you feel better.

A smile will always emit a positive vibe and lighten the mood, so it stands to reason that most people will respond in kind when they see a smile. So, not only does a smile have the power to improve your disposition, it can bring delight to others too. What a simple and powerful tool, right?

It should also be noted that smiles should not be reserved for people we know. Strangers on the street and service people will appreciate a smile just as much as your mom or best friend.

Have you ever flashed a smile at the cashier at the grocery store or the person working a drive-thru window? If not, try it! If you want to be really daring, take a look at this individual's nametag and address them by name. The results will be just as rewarding (if not more) as flashing your pearly whites at a good buddy.

You'll be surprised at the reaction you get, as many employees don't get treated kindly. The pleasure that they get from being appreciated for the help they are offering is immeasurable.

Understandably, the notion that a simple smile can actually make you feel better sounds a little silly, but believe it or not, science has actually proven it! So have a little faith in those cognitive studies and remember that when you are feeling blue, your attitude and mindset can be shifted by simply "turning that frown upside down."

HOW:
What makes you smile? Do more of that and less of what doesn't. It's really that simple.

4: The FUNdamentals of Fundamism

Go for a walk, make someone laugh, eat your favorite food, accomplish a goal, listen to your favorite song, watch a funny YouTube video, go play catch with your child, or do anything else that brings you happiness.

Any one of the aforementioned items can be a FUNdamental by themselves. However, the goal here is to immediately do whatever has the highest probability of making YOU smile. Get to it!

TAKE FIVE MINUTES TO JOT DOWN DIFFERENT WAYS YOU'RE GOING TO INTENTIONALLY SMILE TODAY!

4: The FUNdamentals of Fundamism

Additional FUNdamentals

Below are 100 additional FUNdamentals that can be incorporated into your home or work life. If you haven't found one or ten that resonate with you yet, your journey is just beginning. There are millions of FUNdamentals out there, and I'd love to write about them all. This is just the start.

If you have things that you do for FUN and provide strength, the fundamism community would appreciate hearing from you.

Visit www.fundamism.com, our Facebook page, Twitter account, or any other communication outlet you can find to post your FUNdamentals.

NUMBER 1: Think of times when you were most happy in life. Write down your top ten memories.

NUMBER 2: Find a local playground and swing on the swings. How high can you go?

NUMBER 3: Share one thing you genuinely admire about as many people as you can without telling them what you're doing.

NUMBER 4: Set a goal of smiling for a specific amount of time. Start off with five to ten minutes and see if you can top it later in the day.

NUMBER 5: Learn the names of others. When placing a call to a business or being waited on anywhere, ask the individual you're speaking with for their name. Then use their name throughout the conversation.

NUMBER 6: Start each day with an affirmation. Jot down something you admire about yourself and how you envision the day being a success.

NUMBER 7: End each day by counting your blessings. Ask a friend or family member the best thing to happen to them that day followed by sharing your own.

NUMBER 8: Call or visit a loved one. Tell them what you appreciate about them and that you love them

NUMBER 9: Watch something funny like a stand-up comedy special, movie, or show.

4: The FUNdamentals of Fundamism

NUMBER 10: Search the internet for new jokes or funny stories.

NUMBER 11: Listen to your favorite podcast or one that interests you.

NUMBER 12: Be helpful to someone in need. Carry someone's groceries, lend a hand on a project, or just be there when they need you most. Be selfless. Look to help them solely because it makes them feel good and because you know it's the right thing to do. DO NOT EXPECT TO BE GIVEN SOMETHING IN RETURN.

NUMBER 13: Volunteer or donate to a cause that moves you.

NUMBER 14: Create a to-do list, check off tasks as they're completed, and reward yourself when accomplishments are met. Create a point system for yourself or take time out to reflect on your accomplishments once you complete items.

NUMBER 15: Go someplace you have never been or try something new.

NUMBER 16: Voice your appreciation when people do things for you. Express genuine sincerity when saying thanks and tell them WHY it was important to you.

NUMBER 17: Progressive learning. Challenge yourself to learn something new every day. Research crazy facts, the history of people that interest you, cook a new dish, explore a new hobby, etc.

NUMBER 18: Hang out with a friend(s).

NUMBER 19: Turn off your phone and email for one hour. Take time for yourself without distractions and be present.

NUMBER 20: Be cordial. For one day, say hello or good day to everyone that makes eye contact. Spark up conversation with a stranger.

NUMBER 21: Enjoy your favorite meal.

NUMBER 22: Play a game. It can be a video game, card game, or a sport with friends or family. Want to have even more fun? Make up your own new game!

4: The FUNdamentals of Fundamism

NUMBER 23: Express confidence. Force yourself to be more assertive and sure of yourself. Wear bright colored socks, approach people you do not typically interact with, tell your family something you are proud of that you accomplished in the day, and more.

NUMBER 24: Be environmentally conscious. Pick up trash on the street, volunteer to clean up a park or garden, etc.

NUMBER 25: Write down your thoughts. Keep a diary or journal, and reflect regularly.

NUMBER 26: Let go of a fear. Release yourself of an inhibition or conquer a fear. Ride a roller coaster, dance in public, sing in front of others, or do something you have thought about for years but never had the courage to do.

NUMBER 27: Get organized. Organize your closet, your contact list, email, etc.

NUMBER 28: Envision your future and develop a plan to make it happen. Dream big. What are the three things you can do within the next week to get closer to accomplishing your goal?

NUMBER 29: Give yourself a gift. Take a vacation day to yourself, buy a splurge item, treat yourself to your favorite dish, etc.

NUMBER 30: Pay it forward. Pay someone's toll, buy coffee for the next person in line, pick up the tab at dinner, etc.

NUMBER 31: Appreciate or acknowledge the little things. Smell the flowers, listen to your friends or family laughing, observe how beautiful/handsome your spouse is, and more.

NUMBER 32: Find someone to talk with. Talk about everything or anything with someone in your life. Express your thoughts or opinions to a good listener.

NUMBER 33: Release negativity that's been plaguing you. Forgive a friend or make peace with an old issue that's been bothering you. Call them or schedule a meeting.

NUMBER 34: Steer clear of gossip or negative talk.

4: The FUNdamentals of Fundamism

NUMBER 35: Self-talk. Talk to yourself throughout the day. Give yourself positive feedback, ask yourself questions, or pump yourself up.

NUMBER 36: Ask to speak with someone's superior and let the superior know the person did their job really well.

NUMBER 37: Speak with a smile. Mama always told you, it is not what you say but how you say it. Communicate with a smile and see how much of a difference it makes.

NUMBER 38: Paint a picture. It can be something basic like a rainbow or something complex like the Mona Lisa. Whatever you choose, just enjoy being creative and artistic.

NUMBER 39: Take a yoga class or try a few poses from the internet.

NUMBER 40: Improv. Use your imagination at a team meeting or family gathering, and get everyone involved. You can do an internet search of "improv games" and find tons of examples or create your own.

NUMBER 41: Show a genuine interest in others by asking open-ended questions to learn more about them. Try asking coworkers or family members things that you may not know about them.

NUMBER 42: Hide-and-seek. Get a crew of family, friends, or coworkers together and let the fun begin.

NUMBER 43: Photography. Identify a few places, people, or moments you would like to capture. Try using different filters, captions, angles, and more to add flavor to the imagery.

NUMBER 44: Wear a costume while performing a daily task. Wear an old Halloween outfit to the grocery store and act like it's just a normal day.

NUMBER 45: What's the best thing that's happened to you today? Write it down and revisit it on a day when things aren't going your way. As your day evolves and better things happen, write them down too!

4: The FUNdamentals of Fundamism

NUMBER 46: Create a game at work. Call center bingo, Jeopardy-style learning, coworker trivia, alphabet games where one coworker identifies a fun word starting with the letter A then moves down the line with the next coworker and letter. Research "fun games at work" or come up with your own.

NUMBER 47: Water balloon fight. Fill up fifty to a hundred water balloons and invite neighbors or coworkers to join in. Line up in rows in front of partners and see how far you can play catch with a water balloon without it breaking (this is also super fun with a raw egg).

NUMBER 48: Go for a walk and identify the things you appreciate along the path.

NUMBER 49: Write a thank-you note to internal/external customers, employees, family, or anyone you think is deserving.

NUMBER 50: Make a craft for someone you care about. Do an internet search for ideas or come up with your own.

NUMBER 51: Send a funny meme to your friends.

NUMBER 52: High five the next five people you see and tell them to have a great day.

NUMBER 53: While doing an activity or working as a collective group, allow each person in the group to choose a song to listen to. Ask each group member why they selected that song and what it means to them.

NUMBER 54: Take a nap. Find a cozy spot and get some rest.

NUMBER 55: Get a massage. Ask a family member or pay an expert. I get full body reflexology every month, and it costs around $45/hour.

NUMBER 56: Color a picture. Find an adult coloring book or create your own. When was the last time you played with crayons?

NUMBER 57: Board game night. Invite family or neighbors over and have a ball. Whoever hosts gets to choose the game. This can also be done in the office over a team meeting.

4: The FUNdamentals of Fundamism

NUMBER 58: Grab a bowl or cup and write out a list of your favorite FUNdamentals. Pull out one daily and incorporate it into your day. This can be done individually, with your family, friends or co-workers.

NUMBER 59: Take a bath. Candles, some good music, and your favorite beverage. Men, do not be too proud. I take baths on the reg, and they are WONDERFUL.

NUMBER 60: Share funny stories. What is the funniest thing that has ever happened to you? Task a few individuals in your circle to write down their most memorable two to three, and share them over lunch.

NUMBER 61: Visit a museum and create your own stories of how the artist got the inspiration for each piece.

NUMBER 62: Sing a song. It can be one of your favorites or something you make up. No one is listening to you, so belt it out!

NUMBER 63: Write a poem. Never done it before? Who cares! Find words that rhyme and throw them together in a few phrases. See what happens.

NUMBER 64: Find a quote that speaks to you and live by it for a day.

NUMBER 65: Put together a bowl of random phrases, pull one daily, and use it seamlessly in conversation.

NUMBER 66: Create a competition. Whatever you come up with, energy is created when competing against yourself or others.

NUMBER 67: Text five people in your contact list and tell them what you appreciate about them.

NUMBER 68: Cloud pictures. Observe clouds in the sky with a friend, coworker, or family member. Use your imagination and tell each other what pictures you see.

NUMBER 69: Be present and observe ten things around you at this moment that you appreciate.

4: The FUNdamentals of Fundamism

NUMBER 70: Jump! When something good happens — someone tells you something exciting — you leave work for the day, or anything else that merits it, jump. Feel the spirit of a being a child again and literally jump for joy.

NUMBER 71: Go camping in your backyard. Grab a tent, some blankets, ingredients for s'mores, and a creative mind for storytelling.

NUMBER 72: Build an indoor fort. This is still one of my all-time favorites. Grab pillows, blankets, and anything else you can find around the house to make the most boss fort possible.

NUMBER 73: Buy half a dozen shakes or frappes, and recruit five other people to have a speed-drinking competition. Make sure someone photographs the brain freeze moments.

NUMBER 74: Secretly place sticky note happy faces on your coworkers' office space. Never tell who is responsible.

NUMBER 75: Nerf battle. Blonds vs. brunettes, solid colors vs. non-solid colors, men vs. women, leadership team vs. direct reports. You choose the teams, just make it fun.

NUMBER 76: For your next department meeting, have everyone take a selfie and leverage it to draw a self-portrait. Hang them in a common space and have other departments guess who each portrait is.

NUMBER 77: Bring a blender and ingredients to work to make smoothies. Make one afternoon a smoothie afternoon and deliver small cups of smoothies to your coworkers, complete with Reddi-wip.

NUMBER 78: Word of the day. Think Pee-wee's Playhouse. Decide amongst a group on a crazy word like "discombobulated," and see how many times you can work that word into conversation for the day. Highest total number of uses wins.

NUMBER 79: Create a cardboard cutout of yourself that is life-size, and place it in your desk chair whenever you leave your office.

NUMBER 80: Challenge some coworkers to a dollar store lunch. Everyone goes to the dollar store, can spend no more than five dollars, and reveals their lunch when they get back to the office. It will probably be mildly disgusting and fun!

4: The FUNdamentals of Fundamism

NUMBER 81: Start your next meeting by having everyone share their favorite movie line done in the best voice impression possible.

NUMBER 82: Surprise everyone at work or at home with ice cream and all the fixings for an ice cream sundae party. This makes for a great pick-me-up in the afternoon and gets everyone talking and connecting.

NUMBER 83: Blow up a watermelon in the parking lot at work.

NUMBER 84: Organize remote control car races in the hallways of your office.

NUMBER 85: While sitting at your desk answering emails, wear a giant foam cowboy hat. See how many people comment on it.

NUMBER 86: Partner up with a coworker and dress as each other for a day.

NUMBER 87: Teach yourself a new dance. Macarena, dougie, electric slide, whip and nae nae, or a good-old-fashioned running man. Why dance like no one's watching when you can show off your skills? So many individuals have a fear of dancing or say they have no rhythm. Dancing doesn't have to be about showing how skilled you are, just have fun. The Footloose kids from Bomont had a blast—you can too!

NUMBER 88: Go stargazing. Take the family outside where stars can be seen at their brightest.

NUMBER 89: Attend an afternoon movie by yourself. You can go with someone you care about, if you'd like. Just take in an afternoon show and avoid the crowded theatre. It's amazing how peaceful movies are during weekdays.

NUMBER 90: Leverage your creativity to make up a story to tell your children or spouse.

NUMBER 91: Play in a sprinkler. Don't overthink it. If you see a sprinkler, stop what you're doing and run through it!

NUMBER 92: Have a picnic. Make your own or grab some takeout on the way. Find a relaxing spot and have a relaxing lunch outside.

4: The FUNdamentals of Fundamism

NUMBER 93: Family dance party! Have each family member pick a song and everyone has to dance. Who cares what you look like? The goal is to have fun together!

NUMBER 94: Buy or pick some flowers for a loved one. When delivered, tell them the flowers are just because you appreciate them.

NUMBER 95: Play catch with a friend or family member using a football, baseball, or anything you see fit.

NUMBER 96: Go to the zoo and make up human names for each animal.

NUMBER 97: Identify an individual that could use a lighthearted conversation and make it happen.

NUMBER 98: Have individuals submit photos of each other and have a caption contest. Funniest caption wins!

NUMBER 99: Find a recipe that sounds good and make it. Beginner, intermediate, or advanced chefs can all enjoy cooking a good meal (or at least eating one!).

NUMBER 100: Create your own version of Family Feud. "We asked Steve from accounting the top five answers for the best movies of all time and his answers are . . . ?" This is a good way to see how well you know your coworkers or family while having a fun time.

4: The FUNdamentals of Fundamism

We've introduced fundamism, done some self-reflecting, created some challenges for ourselves and even examined 115 FUNdamentals to help create more FUN, joy and fulfillment in life.

Now that you have a clearer picture of what fundamism is, let's figure out how it looks for you.

Outside of the 115 FUNdamentals we've identified in this workbook, what others can you come up with? What are the challenges to implementing some of these FUNdamentals in your life?

4: The FUNdamentals of Fundamism

What are the consequences of NOT implementing more of these FUNdamentals in your life?

What is the very next step in alleviating excuses and implementing more of these FUNdamentals in your life?

"Sometimes life knocks you on your ass . . . Get up, get up, get up!!! Happiness is not the absence of problems, it's the ability to deal with them."

— Steve Maraboli

WHAT'S NEXT FOR YOU?

www.fundamism.com
www.pauljlong.com

Right now at this moment, choose to be the victor not the victim. Fight through the challenges that life throws at you and work your heart out to find the greatest fulfillment in all you hold dear.

Let fundamism be your guide, the answer to all you seek in life.

Fun and real satisfaction are at your doorstep.

Now go answer the freakin' bell and let the FUN begin!

If you didn't get a chance to read the book yet, go and check it out on Amazon and other online retailers.

This workbook was brought to you by Paul J. Long, author and speaker at Fundamism.com

About The Author

Paul J. Long is a motivational speaker and consultant that has challenged the corporate landscape for over a decade and engaged audiences around the globe—all in the name of FUN! As the MLB Kansas City Royals' 2016 Fan of the Year, Paul's shenanigans have been featured in media outlets like ESPN, The Washington Post, and even The Wall Street Journal.

Through his concept of "fundamism" as well as his infectious spirit and unique take on F.U.N. in the workplace and life, Paul provides memorable experiences as a keynote speaker at hundreds of events a year. As president of the board of Noah's Bandage Project, Paul is an ardent champion of pediatric cancer research.

Paul challenges everyone to have FUN each and every day. So, what fun are you going to have today?

To learn more about Noah's Bandage Project, go to:
www.noahsbandageproject.com

To watch Paul speak, go to:
www.fundamism.com | www.pauljlong.com
Paul J Long on YouTube

To learn more about fundamism and join the fundamism community, go to:
www.fundamism.com | @fundamism on Facebook

Want more Fundamism? Check out:
The Fundamism Podcast on iTunes, Spotify, Google & Sticher Radio

To contact Paul, go to:
info@fundamism.com | Paul Long on LinkedIn | @fundamismpaul on Twitter
@fundamismpaul on Instagram